Profiles of the Presidents

JAMES
BUCHANAN

★ ★ ★

Profiles of the Presidents

JAMES BUCHANAN

by Andrew Santella

Content Adviser: Sam Slaymaker, Executive Director, James Buchanan Foundation for the Preservation of Wheatland, Lancaster, Pennsylvania
Reading Adviser: Dr. Linda D. Labbo, Department of Reading Education, College of Education, The University of Georgia

COMPASS POINT BOOKS ✦ MINNEAPOLIS, MINNESOTA

Compass Point Books
3109 West 50th Street, #115
Minneapolis, MN 55410

Visit Compass Point Books on the Internet at *www.compasspointbooks.com*
or e-mail your request to *custserv@compasspointbooks.com*

Photographs ©: White House Collection, Courtesy White House Historical Association (122), cover, 3;
Library of Congress, 6, 46, 56 (bottom right); Hulton/Archive by Getty Images, 7, 8, 15, 20, 24, 26, 28,
34, 35, 36, 54 (right, all), 55 (middle right), 56 (left & top right), 57 (right), 58 (right); Courtesy
Mercersburg Academy, 10, 11, 54 (top left); N. Carter/North Wind Picture Archives, 13, 54 (bottom
left); Courtesy of Lancaster County Historical Society, Lancaster, Pennsylvania, 14, 18; DVIC/NARA, 16;
Photo Courtesy of the James Buchanan Foundation, Lancaster, Pennsylvania, 19, 48, 55 (left), 59 (left);
Giraudon/Art Resource, N.Y., 21; North Wind Picture Archives, 22, 29, 31, 39, 42, 50, 58 (bottom left);
Lombard Antiquarian Maps & Prints, 23, 27, 40, 41, 56 (left); Corbis, 25; Rare Book, Manuscript &
Special Collections Library, Duke University, 30; Stock Montage, 38; Bettmann/Corbis, 43, 44, 58
(top left); Lee Snider/Corbis, 47; Timothy Hughes Rare & Early Newspapers, 49, 59 (bottom left);
Department of Rare Books and Special Collections, University of Rochester Library, 55 (top right);
Texas State Library & Archives Commission, 55 (middle right); Bruce Burkhardt/Corbis, 55
(bottom right); Union Pacific Museum Collection, 59 (right).

Editors: E. Russell Primm, Emily J. Dolbear, Melissa McDaniel, and Catherine Neitge
Photo Researcher: Svetlana Zhurkina
Photo Selector: Linda S. Koutris
Designer: The Design Lab
Cartographer: XNR Productions, Inc.

Library of Congress Cataloging-in-Publication Data
Santella, Andrew.
    James Buchanan / by Andrew Santella.
        p. cm. — (Profiles of the presidents)
 Summary: A biography of the fifteenth president of the United States, discussing his personal life,
education, and political career.
 Includes bibliographical references and index.
    ISBN 0-7565-0263-2 (hardcover : alk. paper)
    1. Buchanan, James, 1791–1868—Juvenile literature. 2. Presidents—United States—Biography—
Juvenile literature. [1. Buchanan, James, 1791–1868. 2. Presidents.] I. Title. II. Series.
    E437 .S26 2003
    973.6'8'092—dc21   2002153304

Printed in the United States of America.

Table of Contents

★ ★ ★

*NOTE: In this book, words that are defined in the glossary are in **bold** the first time they appear in the text.*

Reason to Celebrate

★ ★ ★

The celebration in Judiciary Square on March 4, 1857, in honor of James Buchanan's election as president

James Buchanan's presidency began with a party. It was one of the grandest parties Washington, D.C., had ever seen. On March 4, 1857, six thousand people gathered in Judiciary Square to celebrate Buchanan's election as the fifteenth president of the United States. They danced

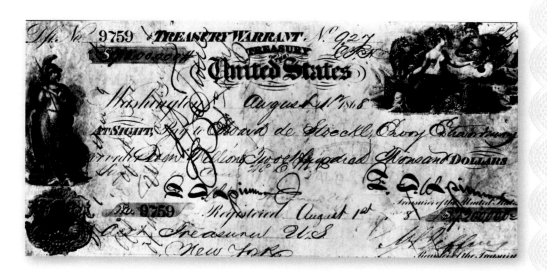

to music played by a forty-piece band. They dined on ham, oysters, deer, and 1,200 gallons of ice cream.

Buchanan had reason to celebrate. After forty years of service to his country, he now held the highest office in the United States. For years, he had hoped for the chance to serve as president. Finally, his hope had become a reality.

Buchanan believed that the nation had reason to celebrate, as well. The United States was a wealthy, growing country. Buchanan was sure the United States would grow larger and richer during his presidency. He announced that he intended to add more land to the United States. Perhaps Cuba or Alaska would soon become part of the nation. In short, the first days

▲ *Buchanan hoped that Alaska would become part of the United States during his presidency. Ten years after he took office, the United States purchased Alaska from Russia with this check for $7.2 million.*

of the Buchanan presidency were filled with confident state-ments and bold hopes for the future.

Those hopes were quickly dashed. In 1857, the United States faced a problem that threatened to tear it apart. That

An African slave ▼ in chains

problem was slavery. When Buchanan became president, fifteen Southern states allowed slavery. Some Northerners called **abolitionists** wanted to end slavery in these states. Southern slave owners resented Northerners interfering in their business. Also, there were constant arguments over whether slavery should be allowed in the new territories in the West. Increasingly, the United States seemed to be a nation divided over slavery.

Voters hoped that Buchanan would be able to hold the country together. Buchanan promised to do this, saying he would "restore harmony to the Union." He hoped that the U.S. Supreme Court would solve the problem of slavery in America's territories. He believed that both Northerners and Southerners would accept the Court's decision as final. Instead, Buchanan found himself powerless to bring the nation together. Before his presidency was finished, seven Southern states had seceded, or left the Union. The United States was on the brink of civil war. Buchanan's presidency, which had begun with such confidence, ended in disaster.

Young Man of Pennsylvania

★ ★ ★

James Buchanan was the last U.S. president born during the 1700s. He was born on April 23, 1791, in a log cabin in Cove Gap, Pennsylvania. Cove Gap was a small town in the southern part of the state. His father, also named James,

The log cabin ▶ where James Buchanan was born in 1791

owned and operated a store there. The elder James Buchanan had come to Pennsylvania from Ireland just a few years earlier. He married Elizabeth Speer in 1788, and the two began raising a family that grew to include eleven children. The future president was the second child born into the family and the oldest son.

When young James was three years old, the family moved into a home near Mercersburg, a larger town nearby. His father opened a store there that became suc-

▲ *The interior of James Buchanan's cabin, which was moved in 1953 to the grounds of Mercersburg Academy*

cessful. The store was one of the main gathering places for the men of the town. They would meet there and swap stories about farming or hunting and discuss the issues of the day.

Young James spent much of his childhood helping at the store. His father was strict and demanding. He taught James to value money and to keep careful records of his expenses. James would continue to be careful with money all his life.

At home, James received much of his early education from his mother, Elizabeth. She read to her son and passed on to him her strong religious beliefs. In fact, Elizabeth hoped her oldest son would grow up to be a minister. Her husband had other plans for the boy, however. The elder James Buchanan wanted his son to become a lawyer.

As the family business continued to prosper, young James was able to attend the best schools in the area. He studied Latin, Greek, and other subjects at the nearby Old Stone Academy. Then, in 1807, he enrolled in Dickinson College in Carlisle, Pennsylvania. James was just sixteen, but it was not unusual for students to begin college at an early age at that time. Away from his strict parents, James spent much of his time getting in trouble. Twice he was punished by college officials for disorderly conduct. Once he was nearly kicked out of school.

◄ *The Old West building at Dickinson College was built in 1803.*

Still, James did well at his studies. He graduated in 1809 and was one of the top students in his class.

At his father's urging, Buchanan began studying to become a lawyer soon after his graduation. He went to Lancaster, Pennsylvania, to work as a clerk in a law office. In 1809, Lancaster was the capital of Pennsyl-

This 1866 photo ▶ shows the corner building (top) in Lancaster, Pennsylvania, where Buchanan worked in a law office.

vania. With a population of 6,000, it was much larger than Mercersburg. In Lancaster, Buchanan met many of the state's leading politicians. On the streets of the city, he saw judges, lawmakers, and other important people. In the local taverns, he heard them arguing about politics. Slowly, he began to imagine himself playing a part in the political life of Pennsylvania.

In November 1812, Buchanan passed the test to become a lawyer. He opened his own law office in Lancaster. Around the same time, Buchanan was becoming active in the politics of the Federalist Party. Many merchants and business owners in the northeastern United States belonged to this party. The Federalists disagreed with many of the policies of President James Madison, who

▼ *Federalists disagreed with the presidential policies of James Madison.*

This 1814 engraving shows the British attacking Washington, D.C., during the War of 1812.

belonged to the Democratic-Republican Party. The top political issue at the time was the War of 1812 (1812–1814), which was a conflict between the United States and Great Britain. The Federalist Party criticized the way Madison handled this war. In fact, many Federalists had been against starting the war in the first place.

In 1814, British troops invaded the United States and captured Washington, D.C. Alarmed Americans rose up to defend Baltimore, Maryland, the next target for British attack. Buchanan joined a unit called the Lancaster County Dragoons. They headed off to help defend Baltimore. The British troops were turned back before Buchanan's unit saw any action.

With his brief military service behind him, Buchanan returned to Lancaster and entered his first political race. He ran for the state **legislature** as a Federalist and won. It was 1814, and Buchanan was just twenty-three years old. He was beginning a political career that would last forty-six years.

A Life in Politics

★ ★ ★

Buchanan served in the Pennsylvania legislature from 1814 to 1816. This turned out to be an excellent introduction to political life. While a state representative, Buchanan met and worked with some of the most important people in the state. The friendships he made

Ann Coleman ▾

helped his law practice, too. New clients began to pour into Buchanan's office. His career was soon thriving.

By 1819, Buchanan had established himself as a successful young lawyer. That year, he met Ann Coleman, the daughter of one of the wealthiest families in Pennsylvania. Coleman's father had made a fortune in the iron industry. Coleman and

Buchanan seemed a perfect match, and the two were
engaged to be married.

It was rumored that the Coleman family disapproved
of the ambitious Buchanan. They were afraid that he was
only interested in the family fortune. The Colemans did
their best to break up the couple. Rumors began to fly
that Buchanan was seeing other women. Ann Coleman
didn't want to defy her parents, and she broke off the
engagement. One week later, she died unexpectedly.
Buchanan was heartbroken. The trag-
edy upset him so much that he
vowed never to marry.

▼ *Buchanan ran for the U.S. House of Representatives to deal with his sadness over Ann Coleman's death.*

To help deal with his
grief, Buchanan became
more active in politics. He
ran for a seat in the U.S.
House of Representatives
and was elected. He served
five terms in Congress, from
1821 to 1831. His work as a
lawyer made Buchanan a val-
ued member of the House of
Representatives. He became chairman

of the House Judiciary Committee, the group of law-makers concerned with the federal courts.

During Buchanan's time in Congress, the Federalist Party lost power and eventually disappeared. Buchanan became a supporter of Andrew Jackson of Tennessee. Jackson was a rising political star. He had become a national hero as a general in the War of 1812. Buchanan backed Jackson when he ran for president in 1824. Jackson lost to John Quincy Adams in one of the closest

Andrew Jackson ▾ was elected the seventh president of the United States in 1828.

elections in American history. Buchanan supported Jackson again in the 1828 election. This time Jackson won. Jackson's political supporters were soon organized as the Democratic Party, and Buchanan became a member.

As a reward for his support, Jackson chose Buchanan to be the U.S. minister to Russia

in 1832. The move to Saint Petersburg, the Russian capital, was complicated. It took Buchanan twenty-five days just to sail from New York City to Great Britain. From there, he faced several more weeks of travel by ship, train, and carriage to reach Saint Petersburg. When he finally arrived, he presented himself to the Russian leader, Nicholas I.

▲ Buchanan traveled to Saint Petersburg, Russia, in 1832.

Buchanan did well in his new job. His greatest achievement was working out an agreement that opened trade between Russia and the United States. When Buchanan was ready to return home after two years in Russia, Nicholas I

Emperor Nicholas I of Russia was impressed with Buchanan.

formally asked the U.S. government to send another minister as talented as Buchanan.

Buchanan returned home to Pennsylvania in 1834. He immediately became involved again in American political life. In December of that year, he was named to fill an open seat in the U.S. Senate. Buchanan moved to Washington, D.C., to begin his term in the Senate. He immediately noticed that the American political scene had changed. More and more, political arguments centered on the future of slavery in the United States.

By the 1830s, slavery had largely disappeared in the Northern states. Abolitionists from the North were working to end slavery throughout the country. However, slavery

▼ *The U.S. Capitol in the 1830s*

If freedom means anything to you—freedom from repeated injustices, from public humiliation, freedom to protect your own children from corruption and abuse, freedom indeed to live as a man among men—you will not grudge the price of freedom.

The suppression of slavery demanded the whole of one man's life. To establish a living memorial of that life is the aim of this appeal. Whatever you can give will be welcomed. It is the recognition which remains to be paid to a man who would accept nothing for himself.

This medal from 1834 and the note that came with it called for an end to slavery and rallied support for the abolitionist cause.

was at the heart of the Southern economy. Southern **planta-tion** owners depended on slave labor to grow the cotton, rice, and other crops that made them rich. They didn't like abolitionists telling them what to do.

The nation's political leaders had long tried to maintain a balance between **slave states** and **free states**. The idea was that if there were the same number of each, neither side would be able to control national policy. By the time Buchanan became a senator, however, people were less willing to compromise. Buchanan did not own slaves himself, and he was personally against slavery. However, he knew that slavery had been protected under the Constitution and federal law since the Union began. Buchanan blamed abolitionists for stirring up trouble. He believed that slavery no longer made economic sense in most of the South or in the West. He thought it would have gradually disappeared if the abolitionists hadn't been complaining so loudly.

Buchanan hoped to become the Democratic Party's **candidate** for president in 1844. Instead, the party chose James K. Polk of Tennessee, who went on to win the election. Polk asked Buchanan to serve as his secretary of state—the president's top adviser on dealings with other countries. In that position, Buchanan helped settle a dispute with Great Britain over the border of the Oregon Territory. Buchanan's work gave the United States clear control of territory in the Pacific Ocean, as well. For the first time, the United States stretched from the Atlantic to the Pacific Oceans.

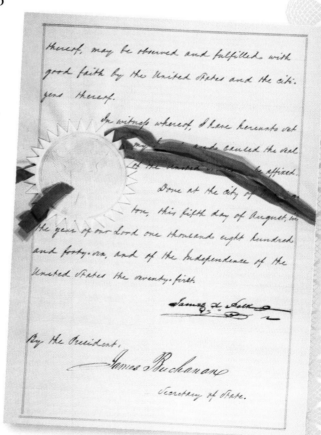

▼ Buchanan's signature on the Oregon Boundary Treaty of 1846

Buchanan also worked to find a peaceful solution to border disputes with Mexico. He was unsuccessful, and the United States declared war on Mexico in 1846. After the United States won an important battle, Buchanan helped work out an end to the war in 1848. Under this agreement, Mexico gave the United States a huge amount of land that stretched from Texas to California.

American troops captured Mexico City in September 1847.

A Run for the White House

★   ★   ★

In 1848, Zachary Taylor was elected president, and Buchanan lost his position as secretary of state. He retired to his newly purchased home in Pennsylvania. It was named

◀ *Wheatland was Buchanan's estate in Pennsylvania.*

Franklin Pierce became the Democratic presidential candidate in 1852.

Wheatland because it had been built on what were once wheat fields. Wheatland was within walking distance of Lancaster. Many people visited Buchanan at Wheatland, including his twenty-two nieces and nephews. Though Buchanan never married or had children of his own, he helped raise some of his nieces and nephews in his home.

Even in retirement, Buchanan kept in close contact with other political leaders. He still hoped to become the Democratic candidate for president. In 1852, Buchanan and U.S. senator Stephen A. Douglas of Illinois seemed to be the most likely candidates. However, the party was so evenly divided between the two that a third candidate was chosen as a compromise. Former senator Franklin Pierce of New Hampshire became the Democratic candidate. He went on to win the presidential election. Once again, Buchanan had been passed over for president. However, Pierce named him minister to England. Buchanan served in this position from 1853 to 1856.

While Buchanan was living in England, the conflict over slavery in the United States was growing more intense. Much of the disagreement centered on Kansas, which was preparing to become a state. Congress gave Kansans the right to decide whether or not slavery would be allowed in their new state. As a result, proslavery and antislavery settlers fought for control of the territory. In 1856, an antislavery activist named John Brown led a group that killed five pro-slavery settlers in Kansas. The violence in Kansas horrified the nation. Voters

▾ *John Brown was an abolitionist who became involved in the dispute over slavery in Kansas.*

blamed America's top political leaders for the violence over slavery. Buchanan escaped much blame because he had been living in England. When he came back to the

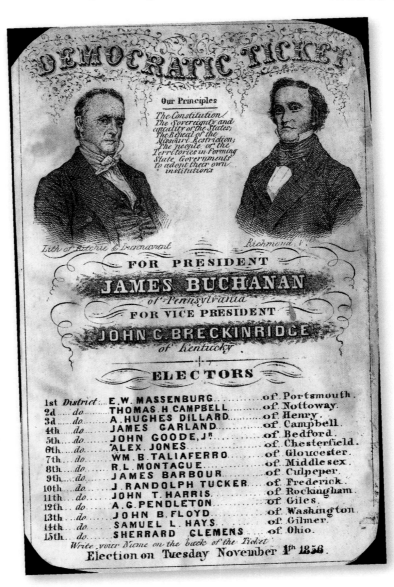

A campaign poster rallying support for running mates Buchanan (left) and Breckinridge in the 1856 presidential election

◄ *John C. Fremont ran against Buchanan in the 1856 presidential election.*

United States in 1856, people frequently mentioned him as the next president. That year, he became the Democratic candidate for president. His running mate was Representative John Breckinridge of Kentucky.

Buchanan was running against John C. Fremont of the new Republican Party and Millard Fillmore of the Know-Nothing Party. Voters chose Buchanan to be the nation's fifteenth president. He won 174 **electoral college** votes to Fremont's 114. Fillmore won just eight electoral votes. After years of striving to become president, Buchanan was finally moving into the White House.

United States, 1857
- States
- Territories

Conflicts and Controversies

★ ★ ★

Buchanan's supporters hoped he would save the Union, but differences over slavery kept pulling the nation apart. In his first speech as president, Buchanan mentioned that Congress had passed a law in 1850 saying that states had the right to decide for themselves about slavery. Because of this law, Buchanan believed that the federal government had no business telling states what to do about slavery. He also believed that abolitionists had no right to condemn slavery. Buchanan thought that if everyone would only mind their own business, the nation would survive.

From the beginning of his presidency, however, the conflict only grew worse. Two days after Buchanan took office, the Supreme Court issued a ruling that shocked antislavery people in the North and delighted slave owners in the South. The Supreme Court case concerned a slave named Dred Scott, whose master had taken him from

A newspaper article reported the events of the Dred Scott case in the U.S. Supreme Court.

Missouri to Illinois and the Wisconsin Territory. Scott claimed that because he had lived in places where slavery was banned, he should be made a free man. However, the Supreme Court ruled that slaves were not citizens and that they had "no rights which any white man was bound to respect." The court also ruled that the Missouri Compromise of 1820—which had banned slavery in some territories— went against what was stated in the **Constitution.**

▼ *John McLean was an associate justice on the U.S. Supreme Court who disagreed with the Dred Scott decision.*

The Dred Scott case stirred up strong feelings on both sides of the slavery dispute. Buchanan supported the ruling because he thought it settled the issue of slavery once and for all. He urged "all good citizens" to obey the Court and the rule of law. People working to end slavery believed the ruling was immoral. They did not think they had to follow it. To

them, Buchanan was as big a villain as the justices on the Supreme Court.

Buchanan's presidency got off to a rocky start with the Dred Scott case, and it only got rockier. Next, he had to try to solve the problem of the violence in Kansas. Fighting there had become so bad that people called the territory "Bleeding Kansas." Kansans had set up two separate governments—one that supported slavery and one that outlawed slavery. Each government argued it was the official government of Kansas.

Five people were killed by a pro-slavery group on May 19, 1858, at Marais Des Cygnes in "Bleeding Kansas."

Buchanan was desperate to find a peaceful solution. "We must end this bloodshed," he declared. His solution was to urge Congress to accept Kansas as a slave state. In a recent election, Kansans had voted to allow slavery, but people against slavery had refused to take part in the election. Buchanan thought this election was valid, and reasoned that the people of Kansas could always vote later to outlaw slavery. Congress didn't accept his suggestion. Instead, new elections were held in Kansas in 1858. This time, voters soundly rejected slavery.

The violence in Kansas threatened to spread to other parts of the country. After murdering pro-slavery settlers in Kansas, John Brown hatched a plan to lead an armed rebellion of slaves in the South. In 1859, he raided a store of U.S. Army weapons at Harpers Ferry, in what is now West Virginia. Brown was captured, tried, and found guilty of murder and treason. He was hanged on December 2, 1859.

To abolitionists, Brown was a hero who gave his life to defeat slavery. To slave owners and to many moderates like Buchanan, he was a dangerous fanatic. They thought his plan showed just how far abolitionists would go to end slavery. The United States was becoming divided North against South, and Buchanan could find no way to stop it.

This illustration of John Brown's final moments before his hanging shows him pausing on the steps of the jailhouse to kiss the child of a slave woman.

A Nation Divided

★　★　★

Congress spent so much time dealing with the issue of slavery that it made little progress on other issues. For example, Buchanan had hoped to add more land to the United States by buying Cuba from Spain. However,

▾ *A nineteenth-century engraving of Havana, Cuba*

Buchanan tried to ▲
protect American
interests overseas but
continued to be
troubled by the issue
of slavery at home.

Northerners in Congress rejected that idea because they feared that Cuba might become another slave state.

Despite his failed plans for Cuba, Buchanan continued to try to protect American interests around the world. In 1858, he sent troops to Paraguay in South America after an American living there had been killed by local soldiers. The show of force resulted in an apology from the government of Paraguay. Buchanan also sent American forces to the Caribbean Sea and the Oregon coast to prevent Great Britain from taking over other areas.

Still, slavery was the main issue Buchanan faced. Even as late as 1860, he stuck to his opinion that Northern anti-slavery leaders should let Southerners manage their own affairs. By that time, however, few people in either the North or the South were taking Buchanan's opinions seriously. He had lost the support of much of Congress, including leaders of his own party. This was largely because there was no middle ground on the issue of slavery. Buchanan's efforts to avoid civil war through compromise became even more futile.

However, one person who lived in the White House remained popular—Harriet Lane, the president's niece. Because Buchanan was unmarried and had no children, he had asked Harriet to live in the White House and serve as hostess at formal White House events. From the beginning, her good taste and charming manners won the admiration of visitors. She became known in newspapers as "our democratic queen." Near the end of his presidency, Buchanan joked that he wished he were as well-liked as his niece.

▼ *Harriet Lane served as her uncle's hostess at formal White House events.*

As the 1860 presidential election approached, Buchanan knew his days in the White House were

Abraham Lincoln was ▶
the Republican candidate
in the presidential
election of 1860.

nearing an end. In 1856, he had promised to serve only one
term as president. His one term had gone so badly that no
one tried to change his mind about the promise when it
was time for the election of 1860.

Buchanan's Democratic Party was unable to agree on a new candidate for president. The Democratic Party split in two, just as the nation itself was about to do. Northern Democrats backed Buchanan's rival, Stephen A. Douglas. Southern Democrats and Buchanan himself supported Vice President John Breckinridge. The division in the Democratic Party opened the door for the Republican candidate, Abraham Lincoln of Illinois.

Lincoln was against the spread of slavery but was careful not to challenge its existence in the South. His election in 1860 alarmed Southerners, nonetheless. Six weeks after the election, South Carolina seceded from the Union. More Southern states followed. On February 4, 1861, these Southern states formed the Confederate States of America.

▲ *The flag representing the Confederate States of America*

Buchanan remained president until March 1861. Confederate officials demanded that Buchanan give up the U.S.

U.S. troops raise the ▲
American flag at
Fort Sumter in
South Carolina in
December 1860.
Buchanan refused to
give up the fort to
Southern forces.

forts in Charleston, South Carolina. He refused, enraging the South. Many Southerners who worked closely with Buchanan quit and left Washington.

Buchanan felt powerless to stop the Union from breaking apart. He believed that unless Southerners attacked U.S. forces or property, the president had no authority to use force against them. Since his term was almost over, he thought he should leave it up to Lincoln to take action.

As his presidency came to an end, Buchanan was glad to leave the White House and return to his beloved Wheatland. Lincoln took office on March 4, 1861. That day, when they met, Buchanan wished Lincoln

United States, 1861
- States
- Territories

as much happiness moving into the White House as he felt in leaving it. Five weeks later, the Civil War (1861–1865) began.

President-elect ▶
Lincoln and President
Buchanan (tipping his
hat) on their way to
Lincoln's inauguration
on March 4, 1861

Taking the Blame

★　★　★

Buchanan returned to his home and was welcomed by cheering crowds and ringing church bells. He was pleased to retire to a quiet life of reading and entertaining friends.

▾ Wheatland, home of President Buchanan, as it looks today

★

However, the destruction caused by the Civil War horrified the nation. Many people blamed Buchanan for the conflict. They said that the war happened because he

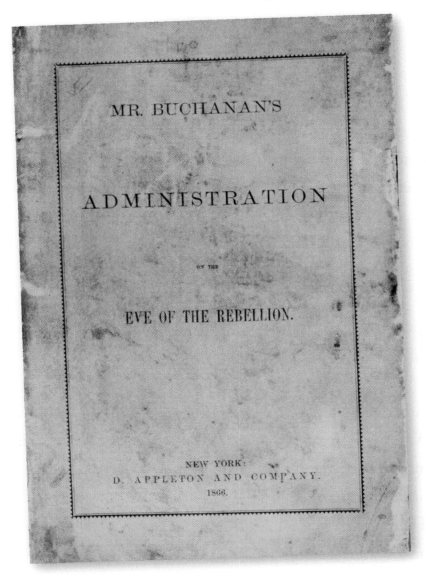

MR. BUCHANAN'S

ADMINISTRATION

ON THE

EVE OF THE REBELLION.

NEW YORK:
D. APPLETON AND COMPANY.
1866.

In 1866, Buchanan ▶
published a book
about his time in the
White House.

hadn't acted. Buchanan even received threats at his home.

However, he continued to believe that he had acted honorably as president. Buchanan told a friend, "I have no regret for any public act of my life." He was convinced that history would prove him right. To defend his record as president, Buchanan wrote a book about his time in the White House. It was called *Mr. Buchanan's Administration on the Eve of the Rebellion,* and it was published in 1866.

> He finally retired, unhonored and unsung. Alas, Sambo, mark thy coming fate !"
> Washington *Enening Express, 30th.*
>
> **Death of Mr. Buchanan—Proclamation of the President.**
>
> WASHINGTON, June 2, 1868.
> The President with deep regret announces to the people of the United States the decease, at Wheatland, Pennsylvania, on the 1st instant, of his honored predecessor, James Buchanan.
> The event will occasion mourning in the nation for the loss of an eminent citizen and an honored public servant.
> As a mark of respect for his memory, it is ordered that the executive departments be immediately placed in mourning, and all business be suspended on the day of the funeral.
> It is further ordered that the War and Navy Departments cause suitable military and naval honors to be paid on this occasion to the memory of the illustrious dead.
> ANDREW JOHNSON.

▲ *A notice in the* Daily Journal *in Wilmington, North Carolina, by President Andrew Johnson telling of the death of former president James Buchanan*

In his last years, Buchanan rarely left Wheatland. In the spring of 1868, he came down with a cold. He died at his home on June 1, 1868, at age seventy-seven.

To this day, people continue to blame Buchanan for not doing enough to save the Union and avoid the Civil War. He had entered the presidency with a long, outstanding record of service to his country. By the time he became president, however, the nation was already badly divided. There was perhaps nothing he could have done that would have kept the Union from temporarily dividing.

Above all, Buchanan believed in obeying the spirit of the Constitution. He thought that the Constitution did not allow the federal government to tell the people of each state whether they could or could not own slaves. Perhaps his greatest failure was that he viewed slavery as a legal or constitutional issue rather than as a moral issue. Buchanan's respect for the U.S. Constitution was greater than his dislike of slavery. As a result, it was left to the next president, Abraham Lincoln, to end the shame of slavery and preserve the Union.

Five years after Buchanan left office, a crowd in Washington, D.C., celebrated the end of slavery.

GLOSSARY

★ ★ ★

abolitionists—people who supported the banning of slavery

candidate—someone running for office in an election

Constitution—the document stating the basic laws of the United States

electoral college—a group of people who elect the U.S. president; each state is given a certain number of electoral votes; the candidate who receives the most votes from the people is awarded the state's electoral votes

free states—states that did not allow slavery in the years before the Civil War

legislature—the part of government that makes or changes laws

plantation—a large farm in the South, usually worked by slaves

slave states—states that allowed slavery in the years before the Civil War

JAMES BUCHANAN'S LIFE AT A GLANCE

★ ★ ★

PERSONAL

Nickname:	Old Buck
Birth date:	April 23, 1791
Birthplace:	Cove Gap, Pennsylvania
Father's name:	James Buchanan
Mother's name:	Elizabeth Speer Buchanan
Education:	Graduated from Dickinson College in 1809
Married:	Never married
Children:	None
Died:	June 1, 1868, near Lancaster, Pennsylvania
Buried:	Woodward Hill Cemetery in Lancaster, Pennsylvania

PUBLIC

Occupation before presidency: Lawyer, politician

Occupation after presidency: Retired

Military service: Member of the Lancaster County Dragoons during the War of 1812

Other government positions: Member of the Pennsylvania Assembly; representative from Pennsylvania in the U.S. House of Representatives; minister to Russia; U.S. senator from Pennsylvania; secretary of state; minister to England

Political party: Democrat

Vice president: John C. Breckinridge (1857–1861)

Dates in office: March 4, 1857–March 4, 1861

Presidential opponents: John C. Fremont (Republican) and Millard Fillmore (Know-Nothing), 1856

Number of votes (Electoral College): 1,832,955 of 4,044,618 (174 of 296), 1856

Writings: *Mr. Buchanan's Administration on the Eve of the Rebellion* (1866)

James Buchanan's Cabinet

Secretary of state:
Lewis Cass (1857–1860)
Jeremiah S. Black (1860–1861)

Secretary of the treasury:
Howell Cobb (1857–1860)
Philip F. Thomas (1860–1861)
John A. Dix (1861)

Secretary of war:
John B. Floyd (1857–1860)
Joseph Holt (1861)

Attorney general:
Jeremiah S. Black (1857–1860)
Edwin M. Stanton (1860–1861)

Postmaster general:
Aaron V. Brown (1857–1859)
Joseph Holt (1859–1861)
Horatio King (1861)

Secretary of the navy:
Isaac Toucey (1857–1861)

Secretary of the interior:
Jacob Thompson (1857–1861)

JAMES BUCHANAN'S LIFE AND TIMES

★ ★ ★

BUCHANAN'S LIFE

April 23, James Buchanan is born in Cove Gap, Pennsylvania (below) — **1791**

Graduates from Dickinson College (left) — **1809**

Starts a law practice in Lancaster, Pennsylvania — **1813**

Joins the army during the War of 1812

Elected to Pennsylvania House of Representatives — **1814**

WORLD EVENTS

1791 — Austrian composer Wolfgang Amadeus Mozart (right) dies

1799 — Napoléon Bonaparte (right) takes control of France

1812-1814 — The United States and Britain fight the War of 1812

1814-1815 — European states meet in Vienna, Austria, to redraw national borders after the conclusion of the Napoleonic Wars

1800

1810

BUCHANAN'S LIFE

Elected to U.S. House of Representatives	1820

Appointed minister to Russia	1832
Becomes a member of the U.S. Senate	1834
Loses the Democratic nomination for president to James K. Polk	1844

WORLD EVENTS

1820   Susan B. Anthony (right), a leader of the American woman suffrage movement, is born

1826   The first photograph is taken by Joseph Niépce, a French physicist

1829   The first practical sewing machine is invented by French tailor Barthélemy Thimonnier (right)

1833   Great Britain abolishes slavery

1836   Texans defeat Mexican troops at San Jacinto after a deadly battle at the Alamo (below)

1840   Auguste Rodin, famous sculptor of *The Thinker* (right), is born

BUCHANAN'S LIFE		WORLD EVENTS
Named secretary of state by President James K. Polk	1845	
Loses the Democratic nomination for president to Zachary Taylor	1848	1848 *The Communist Manifesto,* by German writer Karl Marx (below), is widely distributed

1850

Loses the Democratic nomination for president to Franklin Pierce (above)	1852	1852 American Harriet Beecher Stowe (below) publishes *Uncle Tom's Cabin*
Appointed minister to Great Britain	1853	

BUCHANAN'S LIFE

Presidential Election Results:	Popular Votes	Electoral Votes
1856 James Buchanan	1,832,955	174
John C. Fremont	1,339,932	114
Millard Fillmore	871,731	8

The Supreme Court decides the Dred Scott case, ruling that no African-American can claim U.S. citizenship — 1857

Sends troops to Paraguay after an American is killed by soldiers — 1858

WORLD EVENTS

1856 The Treaty of Paris ends the Crimean War

1857 E.G. Otis installs the first safety elevator in the United States

1858 English scientist Charles Darwin (above) presents his theory of evolution

BUCHANAN'S LIFE

October 17, John Brown leads a raid in Harpers Ferry, in what is now West Virginia, as part of his plan to start a slave rebellion

1859

December 20, South Carolina secedes from the Union

1860

February 4, the Confederate States of America is formed

1861

March 4, Abraham Lincoln (below) becomes the sixteenth U.S. president

1860

WORLD EVENTS

1859

A Tale Of Two Cities by Charles Dickens is published

1860

Austrian composer Gustav Mahler (below) is born in Kalischt (now in Austria)

BUCHANAN'S LIFE

Writes *Mr. Buchanan's Administration on the Eve of the Rebellion* (above)   1866

June 1, dies near Lancaster, Pennsylvania   1868

He finally retired, unhonored and unsung. "Alas, Sambo, mark thy coming fate!"
Washington Evening Express, 30th.

Death of Mr. Buchanan—Proclamation of the President.

WASHINGTON, June 2, 1868.

The President with deep regret announces to the people of the United States the decease, at Wheatland, Pennsylvania, on the 1st instant, of his honored predecessor, James Buchanan.

The event will occasion mourning in the nation for the loss of an eminent citizen and an honored public servant.

As a mark of respect for his memory, it is ordered that the executive departments be immediately placed in mourning, and all business be suspended on the day of the funeral.

It is further ordered that the War and Navy Departments cause suitable military and naval honors to be paid on this occasion to the memory of the illustrious dead.

ANDREW JOHNSON.

WORLD EVENTS

1865   *Tristan and Isolde,* by German composer Richard Wagner, opens in Munich

Lewis Carroll writes *Alice's Adventures in Wonderland*

1868   Louisa May Alcott publishes *Little Women*

1869   The periodic table of elements is invented

The transcontinental railroad across the United States is completed (below)

UNDERSTANDING JAMES BUCHANAN AND HIS PRESIDENCY

★ ★ ★

IN THE LIBRARY

Joseph, Paul. *James Buchanan*. Edina, Minn.: Abdo & Daughters, 2001.

Souter, Gary, and Janet Souter. *James Buchanan: Our Fifteenth President*. Chanhassen, Minn: The Child's World, 2002.

ON THE WEB

The American President—James Buchanan
http://www.americanpresident.org/history/jamesbuchanan
To read in-depth information about Buchanan and his presidency

Internet Public Library—James Buchanan
http://www.ipl.org/div/potus/jbuchanan.html
For information about Buchanan's presidency
and many links to other resources

The White House—James Buchanan
http://www.whitehouse.gov/history/presidents/jb15.html
To learn more about Buchanan's life and presidency

James Buchanan Foundation
http://www.wheatland.org
To learn about Buchanan's life
and Wheatland, his Pennsylvania home

BUCHANAN HISTORIC SITES
ACROSS THE COUNTRY

Buchanan's Birthplace State Park
Cowans Gap State Park
Fort Loudon, PA 17224
717/485-3948
To see where Buchanan was born

James Buchanan's Burial Site
538 E. Strawberry Street
Lancaster, PA 17602
717/295-7220
To visit Buchanan's grave

Buchanan's Estate, Wheatland
1120 Marietta Avenue
Lancaster, PA 17603
717/392-8721
To see the home where Buchanan
lived in his later years

THE U.S. PRESIDENTS
(Years in Office)

★ ★ ★

1. **George Washington**
   (March 4, 1789–March 3, 1797)
2. **John Adams**
   (March 4, 1797–March 3, 1801)
3. **Thomas Jefferson**
   (March 4, 1801–March 3, 1809)
4. **James Madison**
   (March 4, 1809–March 3, 1817)
5. **James Monroe**
   (March 4, 1817–March 3, 1825)
6. **John Quincy Adams**
   (March 4, 1825–March 3, 1829)
7. **Andrew Jackson**
   (March 4, 1829–March 3, 1837)
8. **Martin Van Buren**
   (March 4, 1837–March 3, 1841)
9. **William Henry Harrison**
   (March 6, 1841–April 4, 1841)
10. **John Tyler**
    (April 6, 1841–March 3, 1845)
11. **James K. Polk**
    (March 4, 1845–March 3, 1849)
12. **Zachary Taylor**
    (March 5, 1849–July 9, 1850)
13. **Millard Fillmore**
    (July 10, 1850–March 3, 1853)
14. **Franklin Pierce**
    (March 4, 1853–March 3, 1857)
15. **James Buchanan**
    (March 4, 1857–March 3, 1861)
16. **Abraham Lincoln**
    (March 4, 1861–April 15, 1865)
17. **Andrew Johnson**
    (April 15, 1865–March 3, 1869)

18. **Ulysses S. Grant**
    (March 4, 1869–March 3, 1877)
19. **Rutherford B. Hayes**
    (March 4, 1877–March 3, 1881)
20. **James Garfield**
    (March 4, 1881–Sept 19, 1881)
21. **Chester Arthur**
    (Sept 20, 1881–March 3, 1885)
22. **Grover Cleveland**
    (March 4, 1885–March 3, 1889)
23. **Benjamin Harrison**
    (March 4, 1889–March 3, 1893)
24. **Grover Cleveland**
    (March 4, 1893–March 3, 1897)
25. **William McKinley**
    (March 4, 1897–
    September 14, 1901)
26. **Theodore Roosevelt**
    (September 14, 1901–
    March 3, 1909)
27. **William Howard Taft**
    (March 4, 1909–March 3, 1913)
28. **Woodrow Wilson**
    (March 4, 1913–March 3, 1921)
29. **Warren G. Harding**
    (March 4, 1921–August 2, 1923)
30. **Calvin Coolidge**
    (August 3, 1923–March 3, 1929)
31. **Herbert Hoover**
    (March 4, 1929–March 3, 1933)
32. **Franklin D. Roosevelt**
    (March 4, 1933–April 12, 1945)

33. **Harry S. Truman**
    (April 12, 1945–
    January 20, 1953)
34. **Dwight D. Eisenhower**
    (January 20, 1953–
    January 20, 1961)
35. **John F. Kennedy**
    (January 20, 1961–
    November 22, 1963)
36. **Lyndon B. Johnson**
    (November 22, 1963–
    January 20, 1969)
37. **Richard M. Nixon**
    (January 20, 1969–
    August 9, 1974)
38. **Gerald R. Ford**
    (August 9, 1974–
    January 20, 1977)
39. **James Earl Carter**
    (January 20, 1977–
    January 20, 1981)
40. **Ronald Reagan**
    (January 20, 1981–
    January 20, 1989)
41. **George H. W. Bush**
    (January 20, 1989–
    January 20, 1993)
42. **William Jefferson Clinton**
    (January 20, 1993–
    January 20, 2001)
43. **George W. Bush**
    (January 20, 2001–)

INDEX

★ ★ ★

Index

ABOUT THE AUTHOR

Andrew Santella writes for magazines and newspapers, including *GQ* and the *New York Times Book Review.* He is the author of a number of books for young readers. He lives outside Chicago, with his wife and son.